AF588274

THE MAKING OF

JURASSIC PARK

KENNY ABDO

Fly!
An Imprint of Abdo Zoom
abdobooks.com

abdobooks.com

Published by Abdo Zoom, a division of ABDO, P.O. Box 398166, Minneapolis, Minnesota 55439.

Printed in the United States of America, North Mankato, Minnesota.
052023
092023

Photo Credits: Alamy, Everett Collection, Getty Images, Shutterstock
Production Contributors: Kenny Abdo, Jennie Forsberg, Grace Hansen
Design Contributors: Candice Keimig, Neil Klinepier, Colleen McLaren

Library of Congress Control Number: 2022946924

Publisher's Cataloging-in-Publication Data

Names: Abdo, Kenny, author.
Title: The making of Jurassic Park / by Kenny Abdo
Description: Minneapolis, Minnesota : Abdo Zoom, 2024 | Series: Blockbusters | Includes online resources and index.
Identifiers: ISBN 9781098281311 (lib. bdg.) | ISBN 9781098282011 (ebook) | ISBN 9781098282363 (Read-to-me ebook)
Subjects: LCSH: Motion pictures--Juvenile literature. | Filmmaking (Motion pictures)--Juvenile literature. | Jurassic Park (Motion picture)--Juvenile literature. | Motion pictures--Production and direction--Juvenile literature.
Classification: DDC 791.43--dc23

TABLE OF CONTENTS

JURASSIC PARK

Bringing dinosaurs back to life to thrill audiences around the world, *Jurassic Park* was a **blockbuster** 65 million years in the making!

Breaking **CGI** ground and box office records, *Jurassic Park* inspired moviegoers to dig deeper into dinosaur history!

LIGHTS, CAMERA, ...

Michael Crichton began writing his *Jurassic Park* novel in the 1980s. He wanted to explore the use of science for profit. Universal Studios bought the **rights** before the story was finished.

Steven Spielberg was preparing to film *Schindler's List* when he heard about the novel. Spielberg was so excited by it, he decided to make both films in the same year!

ACTION!

Hurricane Iniki struck Hawaii, delaying the filming of *Jurassic Park*. The robotic T. Rex sometimes malfunctioned because of the rain. It scared the cast and crew.

Robotics and **CGI** brought the dinosaurs to life. The life-size T. Rex weighed 15,000 lbs (6,804 kg).

Sound designers combined dog, penguin, alligator, and elephant noises to create the T. Rex's roar.

Paleontologist Jack Horner was brought in to make sure the dinosaurs were scientifically accurate. But sometimes Spielberg and his crew ignored his advice.

Once filming **wrapped**, Spielberg went to Poland to make *Schindler's List*. He asked longtime friend, George Lucas, to handle the digital dinosaur effects. And the hard work paid off!

LEGACY

Jurassic Park was the highest **grossing** film of 1993! It also won three **Academy Awards**. Many **sequels** have been made since. But none have been as beloved as the original.

Since its release, the study of **paleontology** has steadily risen with students. The dinosaurs once ruled the Earth, but *Jurassic Park* roars louder today!

GLOSSARY

Academy Award – one of several awards the Academy of Motion Picture Arts and Sciences gives annually to achievement in the movie industry.

blockbuster – a movie that is incredibly popular and makes a lot of money.

CGI – short for computer-generated imagery. Artists use CGI to create a 3D depiction of an object, environment, or living creature. It can also add images to a live action shot.

grossing – producing or earning an amount of money.

paleontology – the scientific study of past life that examines plant and animal fossils preserved in rocks. Paleontologists are scientists who study paleontology.

rights – when a work is purchased from an author allowing a filmmaker to make a movie from it.

sequel – a movie or other work that continues the story begun in a preceding one.

wrapped – finished filming or recording.

ONLINE RESOURCES

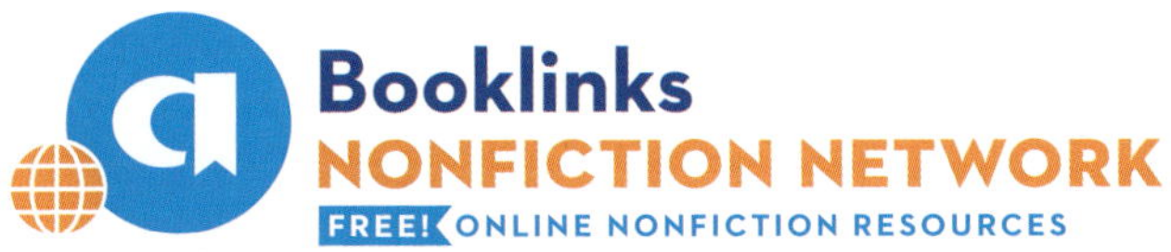

To learn more about the making of *Jurassic Park,* please visit **abdobooklinks.com** or scan this QR code. These links are routinely monitored and updated to provide the most current information available.

INDEX